You're Not Done Yet

Taylor Miller

WRITERS REPUBLIC L.L.C.
515 Summit Ave. Unit R1
Union City, NJ 07087, USA

Website: *www.writersrepublic.com*
Hotline: *1-877-656-6838*
Email: *info@writersrepublic.com*

Ordering Information:
Quantity sales. Special discounts are available on quantity purchases by corporations, associations, and others. For details, contact the publisher at the address above.

Library of Congress Control Number: 2020949764
ISBN-13:   978-1-64620-760-2   [Paperback Edition]
                    978-1-64620-761-9   [Digital Edition]

Rev. date: 11/16/2020

To my amazing sisters, Gabby and Sarah, for showing me that it is okay to be myself. Even though I may be the oldest sister, I look up to the two of you so much. And to anyone out there who can relate to my poems: I hope you read these and remember that you are not alone. No matter how hard times may get, remember that every storm runs out of rain. And sometimes, you might even get lucky and see a rainbow at the end. I'm not done yet, and neither are you.

Dear body,

I promise I will stop treating you like you're a burden and start to treat you like the treasure you truly are.

I promise I will stop destroying you out of anger and start protecting you from danger.

I promise I will no longer ignore your cries for help. I will instead start to give you the attention that you need and deserve.

I will nourish you with proper food, so you can nourish my soul.

I will treat you with kindness instead of punishing you like I have in the past.

I promise you body, things will be different this time

You stuck by me through the darkest of times. You did not give up on me, even when I so badly wanted you to.

Now, it is my turn to help you.

I promise I will be on your side from this point on.

We may get into disagreements, we may not always like each other.

But I promise, I am not going anywhere.

Love, Me

Taylor Miller

Chaotic thoughts cross my mind

A glooming presence making me feel confined.

I dare not speak what I am thinking

So I drown in my thoughts until I am sinking.

It's as if my body is stuck in quicksand

And no one even bothers to offer their hand.

But the few that do I deny their persistence

Because it's probably best they just keep their distance.

It's a dangerous trap that no one can undo

But I will continue to fight and push through.

It's funny;

They say they'll be there for you

In times of despair.

They tell you their door is always open.

They lend you their shoulder to cry on.

But when you do reach out to them,

they run.

People are cowards.

They hide; they take back everything they said.

Funny how they say they're there for you

Until you actually need them.

Then they leave.

People always leave.

Taylor Miller

When I am silent,

I am raging on the inside.

When I am laughing,

I am holding back tears.

When I am smiling on the outside,

On the inside, I am dying.

It is so hard to tell you how I feel.

But I have so much I need to reveal.

I try and cry, but my tears are dry.

I promise you though,

I will continue to grow.

Taylor Miller

She cuts the blade across her skin

To punish herself for all her sins.

But the rush only lasts for a minute or two

And then she sits, unable to fathom what to do.

Inside her head is more painful than the blade,

So she cuts again, deeper, hoping this time,

The thought will fade.

When darkness comes,

My body goes numb.

The sun sets and my mind awakens,

Peaceful thoughts set aside and forsaken.

Sleep is eventually disturbed and ruined,

And I immediately become disillusioned.

But to admit I'm going crazy,

 Is a bit out of the ordinary.

So I lay in bed and wait in fear,

Until light returns and the sun reappears.

Taylor Miller

Her scars covered the feelings of fear,

that she so cleverly had written within her tears.

Each cut allowed room for the emotions disguised behind her smile,

A flood that flowed on for miles and miles.

There came a point in her life when the pain was no longer bearable,

And it was then when she believed that her past was unrepairable.

However, the marks on her skin that were left from the blade,

were not nearly as traumatizing as the
images of the boy being replayed.

It took me so long to make myself strong.

But with the slightest crack, my walls will come shattering down.

It's hard to see the joy in each day,

when all your light turns to gray.

No matter how hard you try to push through and stay strong,

good turns to bad and all goes wrong.

With each passing day comes a chance to start over,

but your hope starts to fade and you lose your composure.

Why does it feel like this will never end?

The answer to that question is one I cannot quite comprehend.

Just Keep Going

You keep going even when you think you can't go any further.

You keep going because they tell you you're supposed to.

And you feel the weight on your shoulders get heavier and heavier, yet you don't stop.

It gets harder, and you move slower, which causes them to yell at you.

You force yourself to look fine, yet they can't see how much you're hurting on the inside.

So they tell you to keep going, and you listen.

You don't stop until you're on your hands and knees, unable to take another step without breaking.

And even then, you try to take one more step. Just a little bit further you tell yourself.

And that's when you break.

You shatter.

You went too far, and now you can't finish.

I light up like a fire lit with gasoline.

Burning all my anger I tried to keep unseen.

I try to put out the flames with the tears streaming down my eyes,

But it's too late now, for the flames have already reached the skies.

A wildfire has started and it is destroying everything in its path.

The consequences are unpleasant, but I guess this is the aftermath.

What started out as being upset

Eventually turned into anger and regret

For not sticking up for myself in school

Laughed at, ridiculed, what they did was just plain cruel

Too late to go back in time and change the past

Too late to stop myself from being harassed

Moving forward is the only way to go from here

Don't look back now, the end is almost near.

Cross my heart and hope to die

Wait a minute, I'm not ready to say goodbye

If I go I'll be set free

Do you think they will forgive me?

My lies are dark and my secrets are deep

They're lies and secrets that I can no longer keep

I need help but I don't want them to know

Do I hold on or should I finally let go?

It's not giving up, I'm just tired of staying strong

Hiding in the shadows is where I belong

To move on and leave this mess behind

I could finally be at peace and rest my mind

Cross my heart and hope to die

Maybe I am ready to say goodbye.

....

But saying goodbye won't rid me from this madness

And to die will just keep others grieving in sadness

My mind may be at rest but the trauma will still be there

Leave behind the past and live in the present, not elsewhere

Staying strong is my only way to move on

To let go means my demons will be gone

I know what I want, and that is to be free

To keep fighting means I will be as happy as can be

Deep down I know what is best for my recovery

For me, however, this is still quite a new discovery

Free as a bird, soaring in the night

Goodbye never felt so hard, because this time, I see a glimpse of light

Taylor Miller

Hiding in the shadows is where I long to be

Showing no emotion, afraid of what others may see.

I don't like to show my true colors, in fear of the turmoil it may stir

But anger and sadness represent me, portraying my true demeanor.

I let out my anger by engraving it into my skin

And my sadness flows like poetry, unveiling what lives behind this grin.

If people knew the real me, they would turn and run

They would be surprised at how much I tend to rely on the sun.

I became a stranger to myself and forgot how to live

To be happy with my being, oh, what I would give.

One day, maybe, I'll step out from behind the shadows

But for now I'll stay put, afraid of being exposed.

You thought you could read me like a book.

You called me beautiful, sexy, strong.

You told me you loved my body.

You told me everything you thought I wanted to hear.

But you read me wrong.

I wanted to be called intelligent, compassionate, determined.

I wanted to be called beautiful because of my personality, not because my body exceeds the expectations of others.

I wanted you to love me for me, not for what I looked like.

You read me wrong.

I'm sorry, but you weren't ready to read this book yet.

Taylor Miller

Stay with Me

Stay with me

In times of sadness and despair

When my mind wanders to the darkness and into thin air.

Stay with me

When the anger conveys through my blood

Spewing out and flowing into others like a flood.

Stay with me

Even when you want to run

I promise I need you to help me find the sun.

Stay with me

Don't leave me in my darkest hours

Don't be like the rest, they were all cowards.

Just, Please, Stay with me

Pick up the pieces of my shattered being

Because when I'm with you, life can be so freeing.

She spends all her energy

Wiping her mascara stained tears from her face.

Covering the scars on her arms with layers of makeup and sweatshirts.

Thinking of excuses for when they ask, "What's that cut from?" "Why don't you want to eat with us?" "Why are you so cold all the time?"

She spends all her energy

Trying to get out of bed every morning and force a smile on her face.

Braving the hundreds of people and tasks she so desperately wants to avoid.

She spends all her energy

On trying to push her thoughts aside.

Distracting herself from the demons inside her head.

She doesn't have time for anything else.

She is too busy using all her energy

To keep herself alive when she doesn't even know if it will be worth it.

Taylor Miller

Mixed Signals

I live my life in constant fear

From your messages that remain so unclear

Are you willing to stay or are you trying to ditch?

You stab me in the back then close me up with a stitch

Hands are held out offering me a bandage

But I'm afraid you're doing so just to take advantage

Your words expelled like a record player on repeat

But the few words missing are the ones that
could make us feel complete

Some days your love runs through my body like a stampede

Other days it rips open my heart leaving me there to bleed

You didn't think this relationship would be so tough

Yet you try so hard, but unfortunately, sometimes it's not enough.

And in my mind I know I'm safe

But my body makes me feel like a disgrace

Images flooding through the back of my mind

I feel trapped by his presence he left behind

Not a day goes by where I don't come across his face

Those flashbacks of him I so desperately want to erase

Moving forward is difficult with him still here

Making my future and goals so far and unclear

So I hang onto restricting as a way to forget

All the times I felt abandoned or filled with regret

A way to escape and feel somewhat of a relief

Until reality hits and replaces it with grief

I can't live this way forever if I want to grow

But it makes me feel safe which is a feeling I never used to know

Once I move on from him I think I will be okay

Knowing he is gone will keep my thoughts at bay

From that point on I can continue to move forward

No more days of fasting, purging, or anything disordered

Taylor Miller

She fights for her life with every waking breath

Eyes closed gripping tight as she looks down upon her death

Hands trembling, quivering as she goes on throughout her day

Being sure to avoid all others afraid of what they might say

Dare they see the truth in her eyes, the ones she tries so hard to hide

They might end up treating her differently,
or maybe just brush her aside

Her pain is dragging her down further and
further with each step she takes

She's not sure how much more she can endure,
until the rope snaps and breaks.

You are the sunshine on my rainy days
But you are also the thunder that ignites the storm.

Taylor Miller

I remember the pain in your eyes

With each of my cries

As I begged for forgiveness

Through your walls of stillness

Thoughts racing through my mind

Trying to leave this world behind

I'm knocking on your door

But you don't live there anymore

The trees around me are growing thicker

Or maybe it's just the liquor

Talking about my suffering

Left you confused and puzzling

You swore you would be there for me

But then you decided to flee

It was too much for you to handle

Or maybe I should've began with a sample

It's too late now the damage is done

My heart is torn and my body went numb

Do you remember the pain in my eyes

As you left me there to die?

I needed control.

I began to control what I ate.

Less bread, more fruit.

Less sitting, more running.

I lost 5 pounds.

I was proud. I felt accomplished.

I could keep going.

No bread, no fruit.

More veggies, more running.

I lost 10 pounds.

More compliments, more attention.

More power. **More control.**

Less food, less calories.

More water, more sugar-free gum.

I lost 2 more pounds.

Less compliments, less attention.

More worried stares, more suspicious questions.

More hair falling out, more teeth rotting.

More passing out, more bones aching.

Less power, less control.

More guilt, more manipulation.

I needed control.

I ended up being controlled.

Taylor Miller

The Mirror

The mirror shows an image

An image you may not enjoy

It makes you tremble with anger

It's an image you want to destroy

It screams at you when walking by

The words sting you right in the chest

You can't avoid the mirror though

So you listen and try your best

You change your outer appearance

To try and silence the critic

But the words just get louder

Turning you into a pessimistic

You tried to please the mirror

By changing who you are

You must realize that won't fix anything though

Except leave you with pain and scars

Beauty isn't shown in a mirror

It's shown through your laugh and smile

It's shown through your wisdom and actions

And how you choose to live your lifestyle

Don't trust the voice behind the mirror

For it is not a friend

It is simply a mask of jealously

One we must fight to end.

It is not the breakup that broke my heart.

It was surviving with you that was the hardest part.

Hiding my scars and pretending I was alright.

Shoving my struggles to the side to avoid another fight.

The shame and embarrassment that came with admitting I needed help.

Kept me from seeking happiness-not sure how I even dealt.

I want you to love me and you wanted me to be perfect.

It led me to dying trying to avoid any conflict.

You said you would change but your actions stayed the same.

Words mean nothing, and to you it was all a game.

Now I'm gone and you're begging for my love.

Little do you know, you were the most toxic thing I let go of.

Taylor Miller

You would've rather saw me dead than acknowledge my struggles and tears that I shed. You decided to sit there and watch while I destroyed my life, shoving my fingers down my throat and digging into my skin with a knife. You claimed you were a man and could help me through it all, except you hung up the phone every time I would call. You told me you cared yet you abruptly shoved me aside, and instead waited until I fell asleep to let yourself inside. I never gave you permission, I even politely said no. But apparently that means the same as "just go slow." Funny thing is I told you it was wrong, yet you continued to take advantage of me for far too long. I finally came to my senses and saw the toxicity in your eyes; I'm just confused as to how you were so taken by surprise. I can finally be at peace and be myself again. But more importantly I feel safe, unlike I was back then.

It's not necessarily a bad thing

To drift apart

It gives us time

To begin a fresh start

Although it feels as if

He broke your heart

You knew deep down

You wanted to dart

So take this chance

And soar through the sky

Spread your wings

And you'll learn how to fly

You may want to crash

And you may want to die

But please remember

Those thoughts will pass by

Although it may seem

Like your world is crumbling

I promise the end result

Will be forever humbling

So take each day

Both good and troubling

Because the life you're destined to live

Is new and upcoming

Taylor Miller

I want to run away
Away from the hurt,
Away from the pain,
Away from all the thunder,
That comes with the rain.
They don't see
What I witness everyday
Flashbacks and terrors
That never go away.
It only stops
With the cut of a knife,
Or starving myself,
Nothing else
Seems to suffice.

Trapped inside my mind
there's no way out
the thoughts growing thicker by the second
until I eventually blackout

They ask if I'm okay
I fake a big smile
I blame it on being tired
and apologize for being hostile

Tired of waking up every day
my mind telling me to quit
so close to ending it all
but something stops me from going through with it

Whether to fight or give up
is constantly running through my brain
my body feels chained to this disease
unable to escape this pain

Ending it would resolve the suffering
which is what I've always wished for
no one wants a broken soul
and I'm not strong enough to fight this anymore.

They ask what I'm afraid of thinking I'll say spiders or ghosts

but little do they know that myself is what I fear the most

with anger and sadness building up inside me

always unsure whether I'll choose to fight or flee

not a day goes by where I question my role in life

the insanity drives me to the point where I destroy my skin with a knife

to make matters worse I have a monster screaming in my face

telling me to starve and shrink because I am such a disgrace

sometimes one day can be easier than the next

which just leaves me feeling frustrated, exhausted, and hopelessly perplexed

why can't I be normal, why can't I just be like the rest

why do I have to resort to extremes any time I get distressed?

The chatter around me seems so surreal.

Yet I'm so numb, it doesn't even seem real.

I wonder if they can see I'm suffering?

I wonder if they can see right through what I'm covering.

Can they tell my heart's been shattered?

Can they tell my body's been bruised and battered?

I swear, I'm really okay.

I promise I'm just tired today.

Don't mind the cuts, they're really old.

Those layers of clothing? Yeah, I'm just cold.

I wonder if they can see the pain in my eyes.

As I sit here and try to cover it up with these lies.

I was told tomorrow is another day.

You mean another chance to take my life away?

No, you're right. I was just kidding.

That was just me being attention seeking.

I'll leave this coffee shop and no one will even know.

And they'll never suspect where I want to go.

I wish I was on the other side of this poem.

I wish I was the people surrounding my dome.

I think I have to leave now, it's my time to go.

No, not die, silly! You're crazy!

Although...

Taylor Miller

Home//Hell

As I sit in my house

I begin to reveal

All the things

I tried so hard not to feel

The flashbacks come back

The urges get stronger

It reminds me why

I don't want to hold on any longer

The screams, the cries

Throwing and pounding

And I lived here for years

It's quite astounding

A part of me

Feels somewhat free

But the other part

Feels trapped as can be

It's almost as if

I'm being attacked

The room is spinning

It looks abstract

No one would understand

The terror of this place

Because they left no evidence

Not a single trace.

It's 3am and I'd rather be dead
than listen to the voices talking in my head.

4am hits and I don't know how much more I can take
the thoughts and flashbacks keep me awake.

The clock turns to 6 and I lie there lifeless
dreading what I know will turn into a crisis.

12pm and there's not enough coffee to go around
staying awake is hard when all I want to do is drown.

It's 3pm the most dreaded hour of the day
thoughts are the loudest and urges won't go away.

4pm there's no way out
the night will be rough without a doubt.

7pm what else can I do
patiently waiting for the moment I have a breakthrough.

10pm it's almost over
what feels like a never-ending hangover.

Taylor Miller

11pm why can't I sleep

I was tired all day but now I think I'm in too deep.

12am there's always tomorrow

maybe someone else has happiness I could borrow.

NEVER ENOUGH

Too loud

Too quiet

Too tired

Not funny enough

Not tall enough

Not short enough

Not big enough

Not small enough

Not smart enough

Not enough.

Just 5 pounds

Just 5 more pounds

Just 2 more miles

Just 15 more minutes

Too many calories

Too many pounds

Just skip this snack

Just skip dinner

Just purge once

Just once more

Not strong enough

Taylor Miller

Not small enough

Not good enough

Not enough.

 Not enough calories

Not enough pounds

Too much exercise

Too skinny

Too weak

Too fragile

Still not small enough

Still not good enough

Still not enough.

It's never enough

I wonder if I'll ever be enough.

I hope, one day, you wake up and notice the rainbow in the clouds instead of the storm that just came through. I hope that one day you can pick out the sunflower lost amongst the field of dandelions. I hope one day you wake up and cherish every hour of the day instead of counting down the hours until you can go back to sleep. And that someday, you will look in the mirror and see everything you have to offer in this world. All the wisdom, strength, and beauty others see in you. I hope that you can one day wake up with a smile on your face, ready to conquer the day instead of wiping off your mascara-smudged face from the tears the night before. My hope for you, is that one day, you will wake up happy.

Taylor Miller

The hurt

The pain

The tears in your eyes

Get louder and louder with each of your cries

Nobody listens

Nobody hears

They just talk over you

For what seems like years

It's not about understanding

It's not about relating

It's about being there for you

Wouldn't that be something

I see you

I hear you

Are the words we want spoken to us

It would make it much easier

To earn all your trust

Tired of writing

Tired of reading

The thoughts get so loud

Until it becomes overwhelming

Cutting, starving, purging

It's your only control

It makes you feel safe

It makes you feel whole

You're Not Done Yet

You want to be heard

You want to be saved

You want this to end

Before it puts you in your grave

But nobody listens

Nobody hears

They just talk over you

For what seems like years

And all of the hurt

The pain

The tears in your eyes

Get louder and louder with each of your cries...

But I see you

I hear you

And I want you to know

If we lean on eachother for support

Eventually, we will begin to grow.

Taylor Miller

Contentment

Feeling content is like looking up into the sky after a storm.

The clouds are no longer dark and angry; they turned a few shades lighter.

A shy rainbow is peeking out from behind the clouds. Not quite fully developed into a colorful rainbow, but you are able to make out the faint colors.

The air feels fresh. The heaviness is beginning to lift.

You can hear the birds return to their singing and chirping. Little by little, their music gets louder and bolder once they know it's safe.

It's not pouring anymore. You might feel a raindrop here and there, but the storm has passed for now.

You don't know when it will storm again, but you also know that the sun will eventually make its appearance soon.

Safety in Numbers

They say there's safety in numbers.

I don't think they meant the number on the scale.

Or the number of calories in your breakfast.

Or the number on the measuring tape around your waist.

Or the number on the back of your favorite pair of jeans.

Or the number of miles you ran.

Or the number of lines across your wrist.

They say there's safety in numbers.

I think you and I have different interpretations of what that means.

Taylor Miller

Two steps forward

10 steps back

I try to keep going

But my mind feels trapped

Patiently waiting for that moment of breakthrough

How much longer until it's no longer an issue

What will today hold

How will I torture myself today

I try to act confident and bold

But I can't seem to put my thoughts at bay

I'm not sure how much longer I can do this for

I wonder if giving up is frowned upon

I'm tired of constantly sending my body at war

I'm tired of always having to act strong

Day by day

That's all one can do

There's not much else to say

If only you really knew

Don't be mistaken

My life is not what it seems

Social media shows a twisted image

To look like I'm living the dream

My life is filled with madness

I'm not as happy as I look

Caffeine and stimulants fuel my sadness

But my smile reads like a book

Some days are easier than others

And some days I can't stand my own skin

I was told I am my own author

But it feels as if I can never win

You don't know my whole story

You only know what I drew

So don't get caught up in all the glory

Because there's more to that image than what I'm showing you.

Taylor Miller

In a time of anxiousness, in a time of fear

In a time of uncertainty, when things are unclear.

A good reminder is to remain calm and present

But don't try to ignore all the unpleasant.

When it rains, it pours, as they say

But soon the sun will shine and bring on brighter days.

We will come out of this stronger than before

As long as we continue to fight this unforeseen war.

The Relapse

Thoughts that come creeping back

The panic and anxiety attacks

Isolating from friends and family

Sleeping all day to hide your insanity

Baggy clothing, thinning hair

Self-conscious about everything you wear

Light-headed and dizzy throughout the day

Unable to tell because you're afraid of what they will say

"I'm not hungry" "I just ate"

Cutting food up and moving it around your plate

More coffee, more caffeine

Starve or binge, there's no in-between

Hours at the gym increase each night

But you can't stop now because your goal weight is in sight

This place is so familiar, it becomes your safe place

That freedom of making yourself smaller and taking up less space

The control is back, it's been too long

You feel guilty thought because you know it's wrong

You can try to stop but lost motivation

Stuck in the cycle, it's a deadly combination.

Taylor Miller

You used me.

You used me for my body, for my looks

You dragged me around like a used library book.

You paid attention to me when you wanted some fun

Then afterwards threw me aside and decided to run.

The love you gave me was not what I had in mind

But what did I know, maybe I was behind with the times.

You treated me like your puppet, thinking I'd do everything you said

The cooking, cleaning, anything you wanted in bed.

It's 2020, that's not the way life works anymore

You can no longer talk me down and hide me behind closed doors.

I threatened your power and stole your show

You can try to stop me, but you'll always be a step too slow.

Cracked lips, battered eyes

Cover up the hidden lies.

You try to hide, you try to run.

But the damage and pain cannot be undone.

You stare at yourself with anger and hatred

Wondering how this body was once ever considered sacred.

Where did the time go, how did I let it get this far?

Where's the little girl who hung amongst the stars?

In there, somewhere, hidden within the shadows

She'll find her place someday, and that's all that matters.

Taylor Miller

Body like a canvas to create the words too afraid to be spoken

When your mind goes numb and your body feels broken

Scrambling to find feeling of some sort

The only safety you have is built within this fort

Longing to find a sense of purpose

Anger and hatred are all that fill the surface

Wasting away from depression and guilty

Choosing to accept this life you unwillingly built

Searching for any and every sign of light

Seems pointless to continue a never-ending fight.

Be more like a flower.

Flowers are not filled with worry nor fear

They do not rush their growth.

They do not compare themselves to the flower next to them.

Because they know that no matter their shape, color, or size, they are beautiful.

Someone will want them. Someone will love them.

Be more like a flower.

Do not worry, do not fear.

Someone will want you.

You are beautiful, no matter your shape, color, or size.

Be more like a flower.

Taylor Miller

You'll find yourself in the darkest of times.

The deepest oceans

Your darkest emotions

The longest tunnels

Your most vulnerable struggles

So remember, when you think that all your hope is gone

That's when you'll find yourself again,

So keep fighting on.

You are everything to me

You are the breath of fresh air

On a crisp fall morning

You are the buzz from drinking

That comes without any warning

You are the colorful sunrise

That rises above the ocean

You are full of mystery

With words left unspoken

You are the butterflies in my stomach

That turn my face bright red

You are the happy ending

In a fairytale left unread

You are the spontaneous adventures

On a warm summer's night

And you are also a nightmare

That left me in fright

You are the blood from my cuts

That cover my body

You are the Sunday hangover

Leaving me nauseous and groggy

You are the giver to my ED

Fueling the fire

You are my pain and suffering

My darkest desire

Taylor Miller

Finally, after many years of begging, he brought me to watch the sunset one evening. Except I didn't have the heart to tell him that it was a cloudy day. There was no sunset.

I want to be as strong as the smell of morning coffee;

As bright as the sun in the morning;

As independent as the moon lighting up the entire sky all on its own;

And as unique as the leaves that fall each year.

I want to be, unapologetically, me.

If I knew loving you meant hating myself,
I never would have fell for you in the first place.

I realized that no amount of razor blades could amount to the pain

That you caused me every time we would play your little game

All the restriction and starvation could never undo

The choices you made after I said no to you

And no amount of exercise ever prepared me

To be forced to run away and fight to break free.

Taylor Miller

I want to fall in love.

I want to fall in love with the way the birds chirp in the morning.

I want to fall in love with the cool breeze that blows my hair across my face when I'm outside.

I want to fall in love with what I see in the mirror.

I want to fall in love with the way the sky changes color at night.

I want to fall in love with being alive again.

Like the moon

The moon
Is bright and full
All on its own.
It shines.
Like the moon,
You too, can shine all on your own.

Taylor Miller

How To Love Me?

I'm not sure how to love me

I'm not even sure what love is

Sometimes I think I know what I want

Other times I'm completely indecisive

I do know what I don't want

I think I know what I don't want

I don't know much

I'm a complete disaster

You're better off loving someone else.

I believe in change

And I believe in love,

But I do not believe

In changing someone you love.

Taylor Miller

Red

The color of roses

Blood

Red lipstick

Bold

Anger

Fire

After a night spent with you

An ending

Hopelessness

Razor blades

My favorite holiday

Your hair

My least favorite color

Sometimes when we fall

It's hard to get back up again.

Because getting back up

Means facing the reality of failure.

It's painful, scary, and disappointing.

And so much easier

 to lie there on the ground

And give up.

But giving up,

Means you fell all these times for nothing.

You came all this way for nothing.

And darling;

You did not come this far

Only to come this far.

Taylor Miller

Aching

My heart, my lungs gasping for a breath of fresh air, my body
from the years of being tortured by you, my mind, the scars on my
arms that I won't allow to heal, my thoughts longing to escape,
the words I'm too afraid to speak, my smile from pretending
for so long, the tears in my eyes trying not to pour out.

To feel something; anything,

You don't care if it's pleasure or pain

You don't care if it pours from your veins.

Tired of being trapped in your brain

Tired of this never-ending game.

That rush of adrenaline, it hurts so good.

Yet no one can find out,

In fear of being misunderstood.

Don't judge me until you've been on my side of the mirror.

If you have been, I promise,

You'd see my view a little clearer.

Taylor Miller

My thoughts are loud
My emotions go around
My will to live
Is going down

Take time to heal
Take time to rest
And soon enough
You'll be at your best

It's not that simple
It's not that easy
Because another day like this
Makes me queasy

Why can't I go through life
Just like everyone else
Why does it take so much effort
Just to be myself

I have this fear
I will not be accepted
Because every time I try
I end up being rejected

This war with myself

Will continue on and on

Sorta like Groundhog's day

Or a never-ending bad song

But I'm told I can't give up

That there's a reason to this madness

And sooner than later

I'll be given a new canvas

Taylor Miller

I drown myself in whiskey and rum

Till my mind goes blank and my body goes numb.

I hate the nights I'm home alone

I don't know if I can deal with this all on my own.

I'm way too young to be this hurt

Every year that goes by only gets worse.

Poisonous thoughts imploding my head

Until it pours into my hands as the color red.

I think I'm in this mess too deep

I'm a walking disaster no one wants to keep.

Am I really alright if I dream about death?

And count the slits on my wrist to match each one of my regrets?

I wonder when it will be my time to go

No one even has to know.

I might not believe that I am enough

But I do believe that I have had enough.

Hell → Heaven

Those years of hell led me to heaven
All those times taught me an important lesson.
The liquor bottles were empty and pill bottles gone
I no longer needed your drugs to continue on.
To feel the breath of life filling my lungs
Was the moment I knew my life has finally begun.

Taylor Miller

My eyes can see right through the lies you make me believe

My heart may have been star-struck

But I always knew to listen to my gut

I tried to be perfect;

For someone who wasn't even worth it

For someone who caused me pain

And made me question the rules of my own game

I waited and waited in hopes you would change

When all you ever did was cause me so much pain

You drove me to the point of no return

The memories we had are now just left there to burn

I'll pour the gas and light the match

And then run away and promise to never look back.

Red was the color that poured from my veins

every time you broke my heart.

Blue was the color of my life

when I realized that we would finally be apart.

Our love was a lie that we were really good at telling

but I was so over the exaggerated mislabeling.

The way that each of your lies

were covered by my cries.

And your abuse was hidden

in the walls of our prison.

I took my chance

 and ran away free.

But to others who don't know,

they sadly disagree.

Taylor Miller

I took the pieces of me you tore apart,

And turned them into a work of art.

The poems I write are not about love,

They're about all those painful memories that you remind me of

I can't say out loud all you did to hurt me

So I write it down on paper and use that as my diary.

Maybe writing will make things less painful,

Although it won't take away all of your betrayal.

Can I hold on for another night

What do I do if I'm not alright?

It hurts too much it makes me weak

Too choked up where I can't even speak

The sky is dark and the air is cold

Maybe news to you but for me it's old

Drink the wine, drink the whiskey

Drink enough so I won't care if he misses me

My body and mind are slowly giving up

There's enough blood from my pain to fill up this cup

I'm tired of dealing with this on my own

But it's too much for someone to have to know

Taylor Miller

He knows everything about me.

I opened up, thinking it would save the relationship.

It didn't.

I cut myself open and poured out my heart and soul to him.

My deepest pains, my darkest memories.

Traumas, fears, beliefs.

Only to get nothing in return.

Not even an acknowledgement.

When it was his turn to open up, all I heard was silence. I tore myself open, I let him see my scars and bandages.

And all he did in return was give me more scars to try and heal from.

How can I have words for what you did to me. How do I explain that you built me up and tore me down at the same time. That you created both the rainbow and the storm. How do I explain that as much as I loved you, I didn't love you. I hated you and I hated what you made me. How do I still have any words left in me to describe the past 6 years. 6 years of love and hate. 6 years of questioning what love was. 6 years of torture. 6 years of you.

My goal in life used to be happy.

But I think that's impossible.

If I aimed to always be happy, I would be disappointed.

Happiness comes in waves.

I think instead of aiming to always be happy,

You have to find the beauty in the unpleasant things in life.

You have to be okay with not being okay all the time.

You have to remember that happiness is like a wave.

You can ride the wave,

But the wave will eventually fall.

And that doesn't mean it's over.

There will be another wave.

Until that wave comes,

Have fun playing in the water while you wait.

I tried to convince myself that the smaller I made myself, the more liked I would be.

This poem was supposed to finish with a reason why taking up space is good,

but I'm still trying to find that reason.

You're Not Done Yet

Your personality used to be so bright
Like the sun rising from the night
A calming presence in this world of madness
Never failed to take away my sadness
Things aren't like they used to be, that you already know
You keep telling yourself it'll get better tomorrow
The brave face you put on might be enough to fool the blind
But I see right through that mask you're hiding behind
Eyes red and cheeks swollen from cries
Feeling lost and hopeless, wanting to say your goodbyes
It's not your time yet, you have so much more to offer
Your life is just beginning, this rough patch is here to make you stronger
It's okay to hurt and it's okay to be sad
This world is hell and the people are mad
The journey to happiness is a long and hard climb
And you must keep moving forward, one step at a time
The old you is still there, giggles and all
Shoulders back and chin up, you must stand tall
One promise I can make to you is that you'll find your place one day
You may not see it now, but you are already on your way
Keep going, stay strong, you deserve to find peace
You are worthy, you are enough. Let go of the
past and your mind will be at ease.

CPSIA information can be obtained
at www.ICGtesting.com
Printed in the USA
BVHW081404301221
625196BV00009B/266